GARDEN POOLS
FOR PLEASURE

GARDEN POOLS FOR PLEASURE

PAULHANS PETERS LUDWIG ROEMER

Translated from the German by Rosemary Allan

With an introduction by
J. E. Grant White F.I.L.A.

Illustrated with photographs

Abelard-Schuman
London

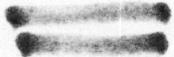

© Verlag Georg D W Callwey, Munich
This translation © 1971 Abelard-Schuman
First published in Great Britain 1972
ISBN 0 200 71732 4
Printed in Great Britain by
Morrison & Gibb Ltd, London and Edinburgh

LONDON
Abelard-Schuman Ltd
8 King Street
WC 2

Contents

Introduction	9
Rainwater tubs	11
Bird baths	12
Wells and water troughs	12
Ornamental ponds	13
Fountains	14
Water gardens	15
Pools for water plants	15
Water plants	19
Swimming pools	23
Ground conditions	24
Construction	24
Water	28
Filtration	28
Heating	29
Underwater lights	30
List of garden architects	31
List of photographers	32
Picture section	33

The publishers wish to thank Mr Edward Collett, Swimming Pool Consultant, for the help he has given in preparing this edition.

Introduction by J. E. Grant White F.I.L.A.

Interest in gardening and garden design has increased considerably in the past few years and has been matched by the growth of new ideas and development of technique, particularly so as far as the use of water in the garden is concerned. Although the larger garden has probably suffered over the past decade with a decline in the standards of construction and maintenance, interest has increased remarkably in making the most of a small site, and water, as a decorative feature and a source of horticultural interest, effectively does this.

In most of the smaller gardens of recent years an informal use of water has been favoured rather than any architectural design, in many cases due to the fact that inexpensive prefabricated basins in fibre glass and other synthetic materials are usually offered for sale in informal shapes. These and butyl linings for pond-making lend themselves to easy but often rather shoddy construction of rock and water gardens. Too frequently this is accompanied by poor design: instead of a pool being designed at the outset to be of such a shape and size that it will fit into a garden scheme as a whole, the garden often has to be arranged around the very limited shape and proportions of some plastic basin.

On the Continent and in Germany in particular, well-built water features of a more formal and architectural type are commonly seen in modern gardens and many excellent examples are to be found illustrated in this book by Paulhans Peters and Ludwig Roemer. The illustrations are of exceptional value since they reveal, strikingly, how attractive the formal treatment of water can be, even in the smallest garden—not the old classical formality which has now become outdated with the coming of the functional era but a freer type of formality which could with advantage be applied much more often in garden design. In addition, the details of construction accompanying many of the photographs, which take examples from British, Continental and American models, are well worth studying.

Swimming pools which have been the one noticeable major development in gardens in recent years are also comprehensively treated. Here, again, there has been a tendency for garden owners to select or to have thrust upon them one of a limited series of set shapes for pools which are offered by trade specialists in this line, often regardless of the aesthetic demands of the site, and it is only after installation that the general garden picture is found to be unsatisfactory and landscape architects are called in, rather late in the day, to improve matters.

Among lesser water features, detailed consideration has been given by the authors to the installation and construction of tubs and tanks for the storage of rainwater, so beneficial to plant life. This is a matter which is too often overlooked in spite of the fact that there are vast areas with extremely hard mains water supply and others where restrictions in the watering of gardens are imposed just at those times when water is most needed.

An interesting section is also provided which deals with plant and animal life both in and out of the water, their interrelationship and suitability for different types of pool.

A study of this book should not only stimulate ideas for more original design in water gardening in all its branches, but provide valuable information about modern methods of construction and technical details relating to the handling of water in the garden.

Rainwater Tubs

Rainwater contains little or none of the chemical impurities of tap water, is usually warmer and therefore preferable for garden use. The rainwater tub can, in fact, when suitably built and situated, be one of the most useful waterholders in the garden.

It is customary to place the rainwater tub or butt by the house wall where it can receive the discharge of the rainwater down-pipe. In sloping gardens it is also possible to lay an underground pipe from the down-pipes of the house to the rainwater tub in a distant part of the garden, in which case stoneware pipes with a larger diameter than the drainpipe should be used.

A tub must be wide and deep enough to make it possible to dip in and fill a watering-can and this is done more easily if the tub is partly sunk into the ground. Old wooden barrels are good material and should be protected with a coating of tar to prevent rotting; unfortunately, depending on the composition of the tar, it is possible for secretion to occur and coatings containing a wood preservative can exude substances which are harmful, particularly to plants. Iron containers coated with a layer of cement and wire mesh or a covering of tiles, natural stone or facing bricks, are more durable; the inside should also be tarred to prolong life. Containers can also be made out of precast concrete in practically every form and are probably the longest lasting. Brick-walled tubs are a possibility but, since, at a given water-level a large horizontal pressure comes in to play, the brickwork must be reinforced in every second joint. Waterproofing is usually carried out with waterproof cement. The rainwater tub is too small to cope with torrential rain or several days of persistent rain and so a gully must always by provided underneath the tub into which the surplus water can run off, either into a soakaway or drainage pipe. A bent metal sheet and a length of piping set into the tub are adequate as an overflow.

If children will be playing in the garden, it is advisable to cover the tub with a hinged iron grating or with wooden boards. Taps can be provided on the side of the tub, which would incidentally make filling easier, and the top could be permanently covered. The tap should be placed as low as possible in order to be able

1. tiered bird bath
2. earthenware dish set on stones

to run off the water: the tub can be placed on a raised base or a space can be dug out underneath the tap big enough to take the watering-can. The connection to the drainage system or soakaway should be placed here too. The provision of a tap will also take care of the drainage problem as all water containers should be emptied in winter to prevent freezing.

Bird Baths

These, the smallest and cheapest of garden water-holders, are too often neglected in spite of the importance of birds in keeping down pests and their attractiveness in themselves.
Bird baths serve as watering-places and baths alike. A location should be chosen that is visible, not overgrown, so the bird has a clear approach and cannot be stalked by cats; high trees or low shrubs will not matter.
The form should fulfil the following requirements: each bath to have as wide a ledge as possible on which the birds can perch; the surface of the water to be one centimetre only below the edge, otherwise drinking would be impossible, especially for the smaller birds; the depth of the water, even as a bath, to be not more than five centimetres. Once these requirements have been met, the bird bath can take almost any shape, informal or strictly mathematical; in most cases, the simpler the better. Almost anything that is flat and non-porous can provide the basic material: glazed pottery dishes, old baking tins painted with a chlorinated rubber paint, precast concrete, natural stone or flat, hollowed rocks. They can be arranged so that they are flush with the ground, sunk into it, or raised on blocks of natural stone to discourage prowling cats.
Inlet-pipes and drainage are not necessary. Small fountains are not suitable as they are liable to frighten the birds. The bath is filled with a hose or watering can, the stale water having first been brushed or swilled away with the fresh water. If the rim of the bath is rough so that it holds the moisture, it will encourage bees to drink from it, too.

Wells and Water Troughs

Today, these two forms of water-containers are almost interchangeable as water is often supplied artificially. Originally, wells were made for collecting underground water only, while the water trough was used to contain water from surface springs and other natural waters.
The confining of springs has been a familiar practice throughout the ages and does not call for great technical skill or expensive construction. A basin can be placed directly under the source, or the water can be piped to a more distant spot.
The sound element is one of the attractions of running water and the water source and container are usually kept a certain distance apart to obtain a splash effect. Too great a distance, or containers that are too flat, will result in most of the water being spilt. The soakaway cannot be used as a drain for natural waters which must either be conducted away above ground or piped to a nearby brook or pond.
Water troughs connected to a mains water supply are best kept purely functional. The trough is usually of the same form as the water-

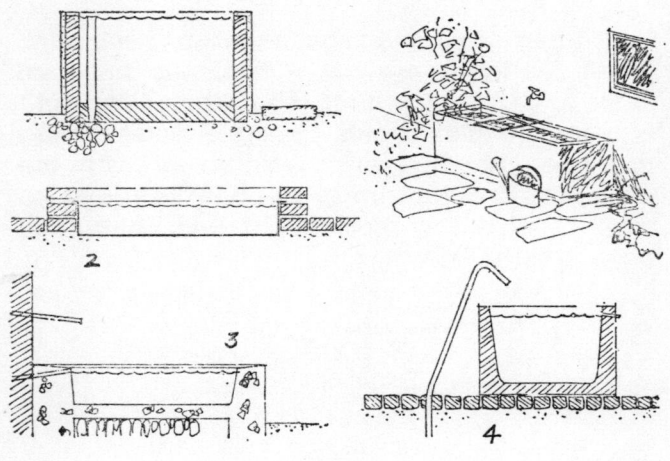

1. roughcast concrete
2. brick-built trough lined with mortar
3. reinforced concrete trough
4. pre-cast concrete trough

Ornamental Ponds

Ornamental ponds are one of the many ways in which water can bring colour and movement to a garden. They can be filled with water-plants or fish and used to show off water in its many outward forms: reflecting pools with mirror-like surfaces, fountains and water-gardens—a complete landscape of water, stones and plants.
Reflecting pools can mirror the house or an interesting section of the landscape. In the choice of location, therefore, the relationship between object and viewing point is of great importance. The outline of the surface is also dependent on this. In general, the ground plan should have a clear geometrical shape since the reflection should not be cut up into random and bizarre shapes but must be recognisable as a whole. The shape depends, as well, on the object to be reflected: high buildings need long pools and when the observation point is not fixed it is better to choose a shape which is close to a square. The reflecting surface must be almost level with the surrounding terrain because deep sides will cut into the picture. Any surrounding plants which are to act as a link between the pool and the rest of the garden are best laid out so that they are parallel to the line of vision and so low that they do not constitute the largest reflection in the water.
Construction causes no difficulties in regions with a hard winter provided the pool has a depth of about 32 ins. In order to keep the pool clean, fish or underwater plants can be added to maintain a biological equilibrium, or the water can be chemically treated.
The walls of the pool should go down to a depth of about 36 ins. and can be made either of strong engineering bricks or of concrete, the base of the concrete being on a hard-core bed. The brick walls should be covered with a waterproof render and the concrete should have a waterproofing agent in it. As in the bird bath, the walls of the pool can be set at an angle of 10°–20° so that any ice will 'lift'. Pools should be left full in the winter since the water protects

tub with the difference that the inlet is not fed by rainwater from the house but from the mains water supply. The supply pipe can be made more ornamental but technical refinements should remain recognisable as such.
Since tap water is often somewhat cooler than rainwater, a shallow trough with a large surface area is recommended, especially when there is a high daily usage, so that the sun can warm the water more quickly. The trough can be placed in front of the house, on the terrace, built into a wall or sunk into the ground, according to convenience and cost, the essential being that provision is made for the overflow—either the drainage system, a soakaway or overground drainage.
A wooden, pre-cast concrete, or metal trough can be most useful and inconspicuous when placed between the flower beds and filled from a hose. By providing an overflow and setting it on a bed of gravel (20 ins. deep), muddiness of the surrounding soil can be avoided.

the concrete. In reinforced concrete pools the walls and floor are cast as one unit and the steel reinforcing must be so calculated and constructed that it can off-set the strains of uneven settling. The stones of the surround should not project unduly over the edge of the pool but should lie at a maximum of 1¼ ins. above the surface of the water, otherwise the reflection will be made smaller. The lining of the pool can be used to intensify the reflection—as dark a tone as possible with a dull surface is best.

The pool can be filled either from a garden hose or from a fixed water supply. Drainage is the same as for other pools of similar size.

1. overflow
2. tiled surround
3. stone mosaic
4. inlet nozzle
5. frost-proof foundations
6. elastic skin
7. compressed concrete
8. overflow
9. pebbles set in waterproof cement
10. reinforced concrete—20 cm.

(1 cm = ⅜")

Fountains

Water, here, becomes an end in itself. Thrown upwards under pressure, it falls to the ground in a definite shape and direction, sometimes rotating, and is caught in a basin. Massive construction in stone is no longer regarded as necessary but as a diversion from the main effect. Basins are usually located at ground level, often hollowed out of the ground. Arrangements of cascading fountains call for more space than a present-day garden can usually afford. The position of the water jet can be varied, or several jets can be located in the centre, around the edge and even outside the basin. As the height of a fountain seldom goes above 6 ft., a depth of 8 ins. for the basin will normally be sufficient. The relationship between the height of the jet to the width of the bowl is about 1 : 2 for vertical jets but, where there is likelihood of high winds, even in summer, this should be extended to 1 : 3 or the surroundings will be soaked.

Ornamentation of the floor can add to the decorative effect of moving water and can be done in various ways: pebbles set in the upper layer of cement, small mosaics, cement surfaces decorated with waterproof paint or a continuation of the paving of the surrounding terrace; there is infinite scope. The shape of the basin with a central water jet will not vary much: the jet is the natural centre point of a circular basin. Polygonal or square basins are also effective with a central water jet; free forms are less suitable. If the water outlet is on the edge of, or outside, the basin, the oblong or square basin will be preferable to the oval forms as the sloping water jet has a definite direction.

An arrangement with several jets can be particularly attractive: a circle of jets in the centre of a basin, along one side of a square basin all pointed in the same direction, or around the edge of a round basin and directed towards the centre. There will always be more charm in an arrangement that shows a certain order in the location and direction of the jets, than in a 'free' arrangement.

The slope and height of the water jet is controlled by a nozzle which is screwed on to the supply pipe and should be about 1¼—2 ins. above the water surface. Recently, more and more rotating fountains have been appearing which, with a water consumption of 45—1,100 gallons per hour, further improve the liveliness; the assembly is constructed with impellers on the inlet-pipe.

A half to one gallon per minute is adequate for smaller fountains which may be in use only a few hours a day. In many cases, where the water consumption is higher, a circulation pump is worth installing, the price of which has dropped considerably in the last few years. These circulate the same water over and over again which must be purified or renewed after a certain length of time; purification may necessitate additional machinery.

The outlet-pipe in all centrally-arranged fountains is best located immediately next to the inlet-pipe in the deepest part of the basin from where it can best be emptied and from where it is least noticeable. If the fountain is in frequent use and the ground not very porous, the overflow should be connected to the drainage system. The surplus water from a fountain supplied by the mains can, of course, also be piped underground and collected in a water-trough for use in other parts of the garden.

Water Gardens

This is the most demanding task for the garden architect. Here, the constructional form is all-important and calls for a composition mainly architectural in which every growing thing plays a secondary role. The Japanese were the originators of the water garden, though many different types of formal pools were associated with baroque castles. By varied combinations of stepping stones, walls, groups of planting, different levels, and the economic use of architectural details, a composite picture can be built up, further enhanced by contrasts between wide and narrow, high and low, still and moving. Streams of water cascading from walls, waterfalls and formal groups of ornamental fountains are all important components of a water garden. However, in small layouts especially, only one motif should be used, either stillness with the accent on the pool form or the reflection, or movement. Major layouts need space, a large and grand area with a technical splendour that is seldom possible in private gardens but more usually found in public places.

Pools for Water Plants

These pools are usually situated in a quiet corner of the garden and should link water plants and fish together harmoniously. Situation and form must be carefully examined to provide the most beneficial conditions for both plants and fish. Most aquatic plants and especially water-lilies need plenty of sun. The choice of suitable plants for shady pools is more limited though algae will spread more easily in the shade. In ponds with a surface area of more than 2 square yards where fish are to be kept, the water must always be deep enough to prevent it freezing right through; in our climate this is at least 32 ins. The varying depths required by different types of water plant can be more easily and cheaply achieved by gradual shelving of the base of the pool rather than an arrangement of the base in steps of various heights.

The installation of a pool for aquatic plants can be very simple. Since the water does not need to be renewed but merely topped-up to replace that lost by evaporation, it is sufficient, in most cases, to add fresh water by means of a garden hose. An overflow need only be provided if the surface area is greater than 3—4 square yards or if the garden soil is clayey and unable to absorb the overflow after heavy rain. The provision of an outlet, however, is useful in order to be able to empty the pool as required. Relatively small amounts of water can be led off into a soakaway situated close to the pool or, in some situations, an overflow can lead into a nearby bog garden and be drained from there.

These pools should remain filled in winter, as with the other garden pools. The fish, including goldfish (other tropical species are not suitable for outdoor pools), prefer to spend the winter lying just above the base of the pool or lightly buried in the mud.

Even though the smallest water lilies can be successfully cultivated in a halved barrel or an 'Eternit' basin sunk into the ground, their full effect is only achieved when they are surrounded by a free expanse of water. Pools should, therefore, not be made too small. They can be constructed according to the availability of local material, for instance a clay-puddled pool can be practical as, carefully prepared, it is very durable. Vertical walls on this sort of pool, however, cannot be constructed. The slope around the edge should not be steeper than 1 : 3 (a rise of 1 yard for every distance of 3 yards). The hollowed-out basin is lined with three layers of clay about $2\frac{1}{2}$ ins. thick. Each layer should be tamped until it 'sweats', i.e. until it is so tightly pressed down that the water it contains is forced to the surface. To prevent any damage, also during filling, the clay should be covered with a layer of sand 2 ins. thick followed by 2—4 ins. of gravel. Any pipes which penetrate the layer of clay are bound to present difficulties—because of their small area of contact with the clay, a water-tight sealing will not be obtained so a water-tight coating of concrete with a roughened surface must first be applied with which the clay will form a water-tight bond.

Larger pools can also be built with roofing felt. If the ground is clayey or stoney, the very carefully levelled-out basin is first of all lined with a 2—4 ins. layer of sand onto which the roofing felt is laid and bonded in three well-overlapping crosswise layers. The installation of necessary equipment presents a problem here. Metal collars are soldered onto the pipes and the separate layers of felt carefully bonded onto them, in the same way as chimneys and ventilation pipes are fitted onto felted roofs. The edges of the basin also require very meticulous work so that the felting is finished off all round to the same height. A thin ring of concrete onto which the felting can be bonded has proved to be best. Smaller pools can be made waterproof with plastic sheeting which, however, is more sensitive to pressure when cold than the roofing felt and for this reason must also be laid on a layer of sand. Inlet and outlet pipes are virtually an impossibility with this type of pool.

Basin-shaped pools can also be made in concrete. The basin, 3—4 ins. thick, will need to have a bed of gravel set under it to prevent cracking in winter. The concrete is covered with a layer of waterproof cement and, to be on the safe side, can be strengthened with a very light, commercial, reinforcing steel or an ungalvanized wire mesh.

If a formal pool is required for water plants, rather than a pond with an irregular water surface, it is essential to have a concrete basin with steep or nearly vertical walls. Construction from reinforced concrete is similar to that for small swimming pools and is described in detail in that section.

If the reflecting surface of the pool lies only a few centimetres below the surrounding terrain, the pool will seem a planned part of the garden rather than something unconnected with it, or even a mere hole. This is particularly true of planted pools. The pool should be blended into the garden as a reflecting surface set off by low-lying water lilies and taller surrounding shrubs. This holds for both types of pool, the regular shaped and the basin form. In the former, the water surface should not be more than ½—¼ in. below the lower edge of the paved surround which overlaps the pool by about 1¼ ins. The surround can be dispensed with in the case of reinforced concrete pools if the edging is cleanly finished off and smoothed down. Alternatively, it can be patterned to remove the uppermost layer of rough concrete. It must be

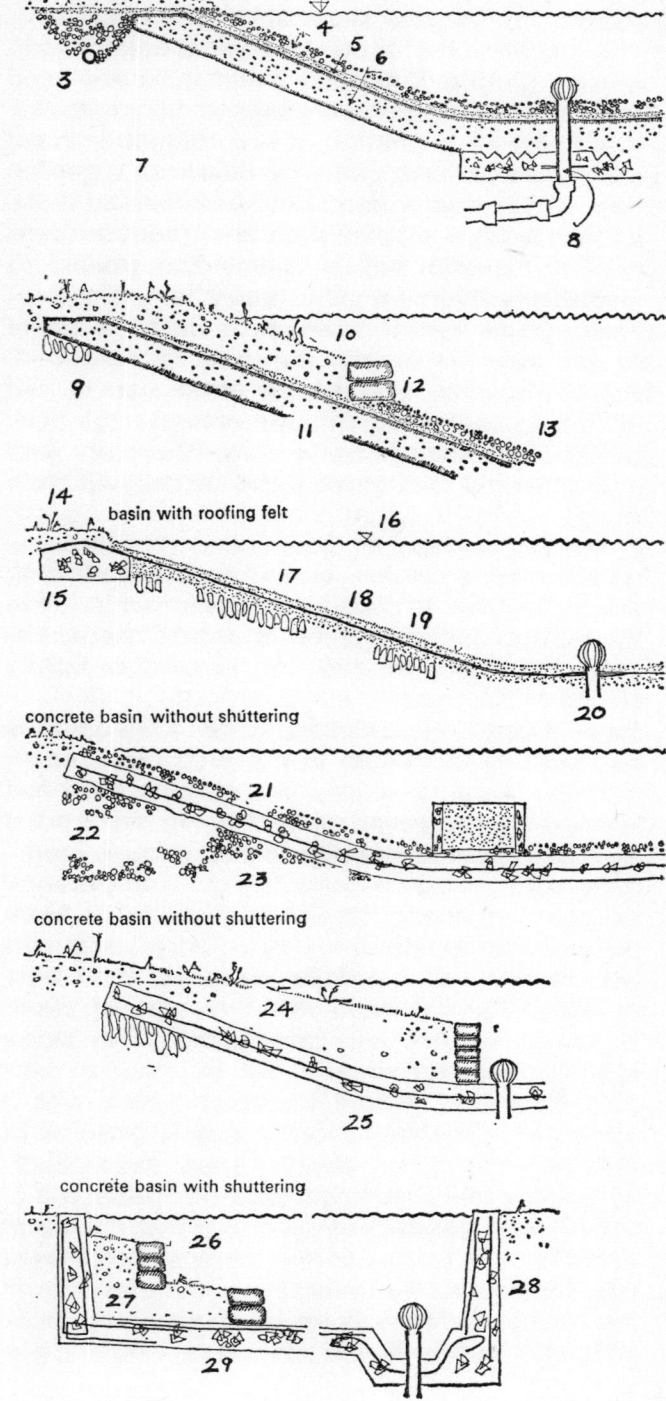

(1 cm = ⅜″)

1. ground level and lawn
2. water surface level with upper layer of clay
3. Soakaway with drain-pipe as outlet for overflow pipe leading into drainage system
4. 10 cm gravel
5. 5 cm sand
6. 25 cm clay in 3 layers—tamped
7. solid foundation via stop-valve into drainage system
8. outlet pipe in water-tight casing
9. clay basin with border plants
10. 30 cm soil
11. 25 cm clay
12. stone shoring
13. 10 cm gravel 5 cm sand
14. ground level with lawn or paved surround laid with mortar
15. concrete
16. water level
17. 5 cm sand as protective layer
18. 3 layers of bonded roofing felt
19. 5—10 cm sand on stony ground
20. metal collar welded onto pipe
21. fine gravel
22. gravel
23. reinforcement: light reinforcing steel or ungalvanised wire mesh
24. soil for planting
25. shoring of halved breeze blocks, cement mortar side-joints not mortared
26. terracing with stone shoring
27. earth
28. in pools where leaves fall the provision of a leaf trap is recommended
29. waterproof concrete with reinforcing steel

remembered that gradually sloping pools have a larger portion of their base visible under the water so, in this case, it is advisable to conceal, as far as possible, the concrete edging and bring the lawn right up to the margin of the water.
The perimeter can also be strengthened with a few stones to prevent erosion, although too many stones can ruin the effect. An edging of border plants can bridge the gap between the water and the land; here again caution is needed if the water surface is already small.
A biological equilibrium is as essential in a pool as in a garden and is easier to maintain if the pool is stocked with fish. Fish live on the products of the water and the plants so a cycle is set up. A variety of other creatures rapidly appear where there is static water. Among the less welcome are the mosquito larvae which hatch in several days or weeks from the eggs laid on the surface of the water. The most effective agents for preventing the mosquitos multiplying are fish which quickly devour the larvae. Other small water insects and crustaceans as well as algae provide food for the fish. Further feeding is not necessary and is likely to be harmful. The fish must be of a type able to live in still water that is relatively rich in food, not living on animal products alone, as do the perch family, but vegetable-eating in order to help keep down the algae. Most suitable are members of the carp family and, apart from goldfish, there are varieties of tench, orfe and crucian which are golden-yellow in colour and which, again, are suitable. The more dull-coloured native species are less attractive as little more than fleeting grey shadows can be seen in the dark water.
Water-snails and mussels help to keep the water clean. Varieties to be considered are the Ramshorn Snail, the Japanese Snail, the Painter's Gaper, the Swan Mussel, and also the Zebra Mussel which has recently moved into fresh water. The snails live mostly on rotting plants and therefore promote rapid removal of organic material. Mussels are living water-filters, feeding off the free-floating micro-organisms in the water. If a pool is set up and maintained in this manner, although the water will become darker taking on a golden-yellow to brownish-yellow appearance, it will always remain unclouded except in the late spring or early summer when the water rapidly becomes turbid and gold-green in colour. This is caused by the reproduction of free-floating green algae as a result of a sudden increase in water temperature after a long winter. At this stage it is wholly wrong to empty the pool and refill it with clear tap water, as further turbidity would be encouraged. The water will clear itself as soon as a certain amount of the algae's nutriment is used up which will take, as a rule, from two to four weeks. No more rapid algae reproduction will take place until new nutritive material, other than that due to rotting, becomes available—usually in about one year. The formation of algae is greatly encouraged by the presence of lime either in the water or in the material of the pool base. Anything that makes the water more acid inhibits the formation of algae, such as peat with its acid humus or small amounts of autumn leaves which have traces of tannin, especially oak leaves or the leaves of the black alder.
A pool without an artificial water supply must be planted if it is to be healthy and rich in oxygen. All plants, especially those which grow underwater only, give off oxygen into the water during the day which is necessary for the fish to breathe. Plants and fish, therefore, combine in contributing to a biological equilibrium.
Most plants need soil for growth, although there is a variety of attractive ones, such as the Crab's Claw or the Water Hyacinth from South America, which float and are fed from the nutritive material dissolved in the water. However, all water-lilies and reed-like plants must have soil to guarantee growth and this must be rich in nutritive material present in compound form and not as soluble salts which will only make the unwanted algae grow. In practice this means that the base should consist of good garden soil which may be mixed with well-matured cow-manure though not with fresh manure which,

again, will encourage the growth of algae.

It is neither necessary nor practical to fill the whole base of the pool with soil. The water plants, and in particular the water lilies, spread themselves out over the water surface and it is always more attractive to see individual flowers and leaves floating on the water than to have a thick carpet with leaves overlapping. With limited root space one is able to control the fleshy, spreading root stocks and thereby keep a portion of the water surface free. It is best to cover just about one-third of the base with soil which can be shored up with stones to prevent it spreading. Cleaning out the pool, which is necessary every two to three years, is made easier if the outlet is placed in an area free of soil. Natural stone can be used to contain the soil but it must be built up 'dry', i.e. without mortar. Halved breeze blocks bonded with cement mortar have also proved suitable. The bottom layer should be laid dry in order to allow the water behind the wall to drain off when the pool is emptied.

Water Plants

Most aquatic plants will grow best in a summer water temperature of between 20° and 25°C. In pools which are supplied from a spring or a permanent supply of tap water, few cultivated plants will thrive except for the water moss, water starwort and water crowsfoot. Permanently moving water does not suit the plants either, especially those with floating leaves.

Water lilies are probably the most beautiful of aquatic plants. Beside the white flowering types there is a large number with pink, red, deep red, orange, yellow and copper flowers. They range in size from the dwarf forms, which need only 4—8 ins. in depth and whose rosettes of leaves spread no further than a quarter of a yard, to the giant varieties which in one summer can quite easily cover four square yards of water surface. The relationship between the size of the flower and the whole plant is nearly always the same so the choice of the variety depends on the size of the pool. All water lilies bloom almost uninterruptedly from June to September. For dwarf varieties the water should be shallow, otherwise they will not develop properly and die without flowering. Vigorously-growing varieties in too shallow water produce luxuriant, tangled tufts of leaves which grow up above the water surface, bloom infrequently and do not make an attractive picture. The list that is included gives a selection of suitable varieties, most of which are readily available, arranged according to the depth of water.

Among the other water plants which can also be planted in pools, there are four distinguishable types. First of all there are those with the same form as water lilies, i.e. they have root stocks anchored in the soil which produce leaves to float on the water. The second group grows completely under the water and only occasionally produces flowers, mostly inconspicuous. These have the advantage that they give out oxygen into the water and so promote healthy biological processes. The third group comprises all plants whose foliage is above the water level, which is mainly the reed type. The last group is equipped in a special way for life in the water: they float freely in the water or on the surface and live entirely on material dissolved in the water. These are the vagabonds of the pool and drift with the currents. Of the plants with floating leaves, only three types are recommended and they should flourish without difficulty.

1. The most universally known are the **Yellow Pond Lilies,** the Nuphar genus, among which are several east Asiatic and North American

varieties, as well as the familiar *Nuphar Lutea,* all of which have partly emergent foliage. Such pond lilies grow best in more shaded pools with cooler water. Their yellow flowers are not very conspicuous, but, nonetheless, very attractive because of the effect produced by their light-green underwater leaves in spring and autumn when the floating leaves have been destroyed by frost. They need at least 24 ins. of water and are very prolific.

The **Floating Heart,** *Nymphoides Peltata,* is also similar to the water lily, with floating leaves from 3—4½ ins. in diameter and 1¼ ins. yellow flowers in summer. The leaves and flowers are formed on long waving runners in the water which attractively break up the regular circles of water lily pads. They must be ruthlessly pruned, however, as they take the light from the water lilies. The depth of the water should be at least 20 ins.

The **Water Chestnut,** *Trapa Natans,* is quite different in appearance. This is a plant which grows anew from seed each year. The fruits are fine nuts with two horn-like outgrowths which sink to the bottom of the pool in autumn and germinate in the mud in spring. At first, only feathery leaves grow on the underwater stem, the floating leaves appearing in June and rapidly forming beautiful leaf clusters, 8—10 ins. in diameter. The leaves are triangular in shape with 1¼—2 ins. sides and the whole plant is kept afloat by the swollen hollow leaf-stalks which become longer and longer towards the outside of the cluster. The flowers are inconspicuous. The special attraction of this plant, besides its daintiness, is a long-lasting autumn colouring which ranges from brilliant orange to deep purple-violet and which appears just when the water lilies have finished flowering. This plant likes warm water and a depth of 16—20 ins.

2. From the large number of underwater plants, the following deserve special mention:

The **Water Starwort,** *Callitriche Stagnalis* and *Callitriche Palustris,* has bright green tufts and cushions of leaves, grows mostly in shaded water and is an evergreen. The water should be about 24 ins. deep but in clear water they will grow at a greater depth.

The **Water Violet,** *Hottonia Palustris,* forms a thick maze of finely-divided underwater leaves and in early summer produces pale pink coloured primrose-like flowers in whorls, one above the other, to a height of 8—16 ins. above the water surface. It prefers soft water and a partly shaded place rather than direct sunlight. It is suitable for depths between 8—16 ins.

The **Water Weed,** *Elodea Crispa,* grows at 16—28 ins. in a less attractive manner, having dark green leafy whorls.

The **Spiked Water-milfoil,** *Myriophyllum Spicatum,* for hard water and the **Whorled Water-milfoil,** *Myriophyllum Verticillatum,* for softer water, grow in long flowing strands covered in feathery leaves which die in autumn. The plants spend the winter as a bud on the bottom of the pond. The water should be 20—40 ins. deep. They are not particularly decorative since the green of the foliage is tinged with brown.

3. The third group, those plants with foliage rising well above the water, can be divided into two types: those with narrow reed, or grass-like, leaves and those with spreading foliage on long stalks. Both are border plants and should be used sparingly, in combination with water lilies and other floating plants, as they are extremely prolific and can very soon form a jungle of border vegetation. A selection has been made of the less prolific varieties, the Common Reed, *Phragmites Communis,* not being recommended.

The **Great Reed Mace**, *Typha Latifolia*, is also only to be used with large expanses of water. The variety *Typha Angustifolia* has foliage that can reach to a height of two yards but is more dainty and slimmer than the common Reed Mace. The *Typha Laxmannii* which comes from the east is rather less tall but is not common.

Of all the reed-type plants, the **Flowering Rush**, *Butomus Umbellatus*, is the most suitable for small ponds. Its slim, graceful leaves rise to a height of about one yard above the water and in summer bear fine umbels of pink blossoms. It grows best in 6—8 ins. of water although it can support a depth of 20 ins.

The **Yellow Water Flag**, *Iris Pseudacorus*, has bright green reed-like foliage about 1¼ ins. wide and grows to a height of 36 ins. Unfortunately, the beautiful yellow flowers that blossom in June are not very plentiful especially when grown as a water plant. It can be planted in up to 14 ins. of water but grows better in ordinary moist garden soil. Two other types of iris are suitable for very shallow water up to 4 ins., *Iris Laevigata* and *Iris Versicolor*, and they have violet-coloured blooms.

The **Japanese Water Iris**, *Iris Kaempferi*, is in a class of its own. This is an old east Asiatic garden plant and is cultivated there in a large number of varieties with flowers ranging from purest white through various shades of lilac and purple to deep violet. Each year in June when the irises bloom, they are visited by thousands of Japanese. The stems are about 28 ins. high with reed-like leaves and the flowers differ in form from those of the ordinary Flag Iris, spreading out to form a large flat plate with a diameter of about 4—6 ins. The Japanese Water Iris, however, is somewhat more demanding than all other water and bog plants. It must have soil absolutely free of lime and must be treated every year with lime-free compost or rotted cow-manure. Although they will also grow well in water at a depth of 2—4 ins. (in Japan they are cultivated like rice), it is better to grow them in very damp ground rather than shallow water. In winter the roots should be kept as dry as possible.

Among the non reed-like plants of this group, the North American **Golden Club**, *Orontium Aquaticum*, is very pretty. This has spoon-shaped leaves, some of which float and some of which rise above the water, with white inflorescence in May. It prefers warmth, needs protection in winter, and grows best in 12 ins. of water. The Golden Club belongs to the Arum family.

The **Water Arum** or **Bog Arum**, *Calla Palustris*, has similarly shaped leaves and greenish inflorescence surrounded by a striking white sheath. After flowering in May or June, bright red berries appear in a tightly-packed cluster. They require marshy soil free of lime and, at the most, 8 ins. of water.

The **Marsh Trefoil**, *Menuanthes Trifoliata*, with rich green leaves standing erect, flowers in the early part of the year and, soon after, its fringed pale pink flowers give way to a cluster of berries. It thrives equally well in soil that is just damp and in water up to 10 ins. deep.

The **Arrowhead**, *Sagittaria Sagittifolia*, has, as its name suggests, arrow-shaped leaves on stems about 16 ins. high. It blooms in summer and the flowers are white with red colourings. This plant, which so consistently shows groups of three three-pointed leaves, triangular stem, three-petalled flowers in groups of three, is one of the prettiest plants for depths of 4—16 ins., although it can quickly spread and get out of

Suitable Varieties of Water Lily

Name		Depth of water in ins.	Colour	Remarks
Nymphaea	tetragona	2—6	White	Charming miniature, often spreads abundantly
Nymphaea	'Helvola'	6—8	Yellow	Leaves flecked with brown, prolific flowerer
Nymphaea	'Indiana'	6—8	Orange to copper	Brown flecked leaves
Nymphaea	'Aurora'	8—20	Copper-pink	Prolific flowerer
Nymphaea	'Granat'	8—20	Garnet red	Large flowers
Nymphaea	'Laydeckeri Lilacea'	8—20	Mauve pink and carmine	
Nymphaea	'Ellisiana'	12—24	Carmine red	Free flowering
Nymphaea	'Odalisque'	12—24	Deep pink	Delicately perfumed
Nymphaea	'Marliacea Albida'	16—32	White	Perfumed
Nymphaea	'Sunrise'	16—32	Yellow	For warm water, needs protection in winter
Nymphaea	'James Brydon'	16—40	Dark cherry red	One of the most beautiful hardy varieties
Nymphaea	'Marliacea Chromatella'	24—48	Pale yellow	Flecked leaves, the hardiest yellow variety
Nymphaea	'Charles de Meurville'	24—60	Inside wine-red, outside whitish	Large and free flowering
Nymphaea	'Marliacea Rosea'	28—72	Light pink	Vigorous grower
Nymphaea	'Virginalis'	28—72	White	Large flowers and vigorous grower
Nymphaea	'Postlinberg'	28—80	White	Magnificent in every way

hand if not occasionally pruned.

The **Mare's Tail**, *Hippuris Vulgaris*, is unusual in appearance. The 8—12 ins. tall stems with circles of narrow leaves look like small Christmas trees above the water. The foliage continues underwater but is somewhat longer. It is particularly attractive in the colder part of the year when most of the other plants which grow above the water are dead. It is best in 16—18 ins. of water but will grow in up to 32 ins.

4. There is a large and interesting group of plants which swim freely in the water, although many varieties have to be eliminated, for example Duck-weed, as they multiply so rapidly that they would cover the whole pond in a short time.

The **Frog's Bit**, *Hydrocharis Morsus-ranae*, requires soft water with as little lime as possible, in which it will grow abundantly. Its round, floating leaves ($\frac{3}{4}$ in.—3 ins. in diameter) and its arrowhead-like flowers are very attractive in conjunction with other water plants.

The **Water Soldier** or **Crab's Claw**, *Stratiotes*

Aloides, has a peculiar shape of its own. With its spiky sword-shaped leaves, 8—14 ins. long in the form of a rosette, it is almost like an Aloe or a narrow-leaved Agave. This also thrives only in soft marshy water and should, if possible, be cultivated on its own to bring out the full effect. In spring the leaf rosettes rise slowly from the bottom of the pool until they are half out of the water, and then the white flowers open. It sends out runners, producing new rosettes which, in the autumn, sink under the water and can be admired during the whole of the winter. Warm and shady pools are ideal for the Water Hyacinth, *Eichhornia Crassipes.* They are not hardy plants since they come from tropical America but their floating leaf-rosettes with round, swollen leaf-stalks and fine pale lilac flowers with yellow markings on their 8 ins. high panicles are so beautiful that it is worth the trouble of transferring them to preserving jars in water or damp mud and keeping them warm with plenty of light over the winter.

Swimming Pools

General

In our temperate climate swimming and paddling pools must be planned so that they obtain as much sun and shelter from the winds as possible. It is therefore advisable to plant trees and bushes to the north of the pool, although not so near that roots can damage the structure or leaves fall onto the water. Protection from wind can also be provided by portable screens made of moulded glass, rush matting, or plastic which lets sunlight through; these have the advantage of ensuring privacy. Solid walls are especially suitable because, correctly placed, they will re-emit the warmth of the sun in the evenings.

The depth of the pool will depend on its purpose. Paddling pools for small children should not be deeper than about 14 ins., so construction can be similar to the pools for water plants. Swimming pools require a minimum depth of 3 ft. for swimming, 6 ft. for diving from the edge and 7—8 ft. if a diving board is to be used. For those who want to swim energetically the pool should be oblong, a width of 14 ft. being adequate. To compensate for ice pressure, walls are often built with a slope of 10°.

The area around the pool must be hard and clean. Paving is ideal and there is a wide selection in natural and reconstituted stone available. Perhaps the best method of edging is with specially made hand-hold coping-stones which are laid with a 1 : 50 slope so that the water flows away from the pool.

In some cases a footbath is made near the pool. A depth of 6 ins. and a width of 28 ins. is enough for this. The water inlet is usually in the form of a shower, the outlet going direct to the drainage system or a soakaway. The expense of installing a footbath is unnecessary with most private pools where there is no likelihood of contamination.

Some people like to design pools without a hard surround and plant grass right up to the edge of the pool. This may be a satisfactory lily-pond layout but with swimming pools, once the grass has become soggy, bare patches of muddy earth result. In addition, it is difficult to prevent grass from falling into the pool when mowing. One can always experiment with levels: paving above the level of the lawn and leading down to it with a dwarf wall, or vice versa.

The higher the water level in a pool, the more attractive the effect. The level can be controlled by skimmers and should be about $3\frac{1}{2}$ ins. below the edging stone. A high water level also provides a safety factor, making exit from the pool easier at any point.

Most pools are filled from a garden hose but a

permanent filling spigot can be placed under a diving board, for instance, or anywhere out of the way. An automatic topping-up system with ball-valve can also be fitted up though, here, the tank must be dosed from time to time with a small amount of chlorine to prevent green growths.

Ground Conditions

A swimming pool contractor with modern excavators and a plant can cut an accurate hole for a pool almost anywhere, though the cost will vary if the following conditions occur:

1 Underground obstructions

(a) This can be in the form of services for water, gas, electricity, telephone or drains. Old wells or disused cesspits can also turn up unexpectedly. The local authority, deeds to the property, or architect's drawings are sources of information. In many places construction must be kept to 6 or more feet within the boundary so it is advisable to send a sketch plan to the local authority before starting a large excavation. Permission to fill the pool must also be obtained if mains water is to be used. The local authority may also ask to be advised should the pool be emptied.

(b) Old foundations and rock outcrops may need a road drill to break them up.

2 Raising of the natural earth level

This can have been raised by soil or 'fill', sometimes to a depth of several feet. The walls of a hole dug in such ground are always liable to cave in even though the altered level may have appeared firm over a number of years; the pool should rest on solid earth.

3 Water conditions

(a) A water table can be encountered even at the top of a hill and would require a dewatering plant to pump the hole clear of water during excavation, installation and finishing of the swimming pool.

(b) Where a strata of wet sand occurs in the dig, the sand will run out into the excavation, forming a void in the wall which causes the earth above to sink and collapse into the hole.

(c) Water-bearing clay areas can be troublesome and should be tackled after a spell of dry weather.

4 Expansive soils

Also known as adobe soils, they do not readily absorb moisture but, when they do so, will expand and create considerable pressure.

5 Corrosive soils

Some areas of soil have a high sulphate content which can corrode many materials, including plastics, fibreglass and concrete. It is a comparatively rare hazard, however, and can be counteracted by sulphate-resisting concretes which are readily available.

If reasonable care is taken in the siting of the pool, most of these difficulties can be avoided. Hard sand, chalk and some types of clay will give a trouble-free excavation.

In nearly every case it is more economical to have the excavated soil taken to a tip rather than using it to make a rockery or a bank: the earth is subsoil and would not be fertile for some time.

Construction

The type of pool and method of construction will depend on financial considerations, ground conditions, and whether or not a durable fixture is required. The following methods are available in ascending order of merit and long-term durability:

Out-of-ground metal tanks with plastic liners;
Out-of-ground wooden-walled tanks with plastic liners;
In-ground pools as in the above;
Concrete block walls and sand bottom, with plastic liners;
Aluminium and steel pool shells;
Fibreglass single-piece or joined sectional shells;
Block construction walls with steel reinforcing and reinforced concrete walls;
Gunite, a pneumatically applied mixture of sand and cement forming a dense high-strength ferro-

concrete, with steel reinforced walls and floor; Drypack plasticised patent concrete with steel reinforced walls and floor.

Combinations of the above methods, with shuttering to form walls and vibrators to pack and increase the density of the concrete, are used in special conditions and on very large pools.

1 Out-of-ground plastic-liner pools with metal or wooden walls

These are the simplest form of owner-built pools. Full instructions come with the kit but care must be taken to remove sharp objects from the level site so the plastic is not punctured. Also a 3—4 ins. layer of smooth well-consolidated sand should be put down. About 5 yards of sand is needed for a 30 ft by 15 ft pool. The sand prevents black stains from rotting vegetation, notably dandelions, spoiling the appearance of the plastic liner. This type can be dismantled and moved to a new site.

2 In-ground plastic-liner pools with metal or wooden walls

Whenever possible a machine should be used for excavation as it is so much quicker: by hand it takes six men about two weeks to dig out a fair-sized pool. The hole is dug oversize for ease of construction and soil is back-filled in the space while the pool is filled with water. The back-fill forms the major support for the walls and should be compacted every 6 ins. to avoid settling which would weaken the walls and spoil any paving surround.

Installing the liner is best done on a warm day with plenty of hands to help. The wrinkles and folds should be allowed to ease out while the manufacturer's instructions are once again examined. The liner will stretch into position as the water fills the pool and should have no wrinkles. Tension should only be applied to the walls when the bottom is covered with water to hold the liner. As the water rises to each fitting these should be set into position and only then should the necessary holes be cut, to avoid cutting them in the wrong position. A vacuum cleaner is a great help to get the liner walls smoothed out when the floor has been completely covered with water.

3 Concrete block walls and plastic-liner pools

The construction is essentially the same as for concrete block construction pools (see paragraph 6).

4 Aluminium pools and steel pool shells

These are designed to be free-standing and can be set partially or completely underground. They are used for problem sites, at the top of hills for example or on stilts on the side of a hill. Each pool would be planned and installed by an engineer. The parts are factory-made and then bolted or welded together on site.

5 Fibreglass pools

They have a skin of about $\frac{3}{16}$ in. and, if properly installed, can give years of carefree use. The surfaces are smooth and do not need painting. These pools are not free-standing so ground conditions must be taken into account. It may be advisable to back-fill with a weak mixture of concrete or even to use steel to toughen the sides against expansive soils such as clay. When emptying it may be advisable to put beams across to hold the walls. There were difficulties with the pigmentation factor in the first of these models as the blue colour faded in time, leaving brown mottled patches, and the smooth gel coating was affected by scrubbing with chemicals to remove algae. Today, these problems have been largely overcome and the result is a pleasant and carefree pool.

6 Block construction pools

This is probably the easiest permanent type of pool for the owner-builder as blocks can be set up gradually, at evenings and weekends. The basic procedure is to excavate 15 ins. below the depth required for the finished pool, put in a bed of rejects, broken bricks or stone, for underpool drainage and cover this with viscoene plastic sheeting to prevent the concrete seeping into the porous bed. Mild ½ in. steel bars, held at the base by bricks or special 'chairs', should be put in to form squares of 12 ins. then the concrete (1 : 2½ : 3½ mix) should be poured in one piece to form the floor; however, some 12 ins. of steel should come from the perimeter of the floor to couple with the vertical steel rods in the walls. The blocks for the walls are usually about 18 ins. by 9 ins. high by 9 ins. wide with two 4 ins. square holes. Successive rows of blocks are offset to overlap and ½ in. steel rods are coupled to the steel from the floor. The blocks are lowered over the rods and the 4 ins. holes packed with concrete (1 : 2 : 2 mix). A ⅝ in. steel rod can be built in horizontally on each course of blocks for extra strength. The block work should stop 12 ins. below paving level and a 12 ins. by 12 ins. concrete ring bondbeam formed all around the top of the pool. The edge of the pool can then have special 'hand-hold' coping stones laid on top of the bondbeam. The space behind the walls must be well back-filled and compacted every 6 ins. If this is not well done it could cause sinking in the paving surround or inadequate support for the pool walls.

Complete kits of inlets, skimmers, sump pots, pipe work, filters, underwater lights, and in-structions for buying the right amount of concrete blocks, steel, cement and sand are obtainable from pool companies who specialize in this type of service.

The interior is finished by a waterproof render on walls and floor and then either painted or plastered with a waterproof white cement and marble-chippings finish known as Marbelite.

7 Gunite

This is one of the methods for the professional only. It produces a single-piece or monolithic shell with no joints. The concrete is impervious to water so no frost can attack it, which is not the case with some blocks used to build pools. The excavation is cut to limits within 1—2 ins. and the earth walls are used as the back-shuttering for the concrete. The advantage of this is that there is no back-filling to be done and the paving will be on solid ground. The bottom is spread with 4 ins. rejects for under-pool drainage and then covered with viscoene and steeled. The steel preferred is deformed high-tensile steel (yield strength 60,000 lbs. per sq. in.) wired together at 12 ins., 9 ins. or 6 ins. centres (this will form a steel meshwork of 12 ins., 9 ins. or 6 ins. squares) depending on the depth of the pool and ground conditions. The steel is set away from the walls and floor so that it will lie 2 ins. under the surface of the concrete face. Steeling in the corner of pools must be carried out carefully. Where it bends to continue across the floor a fan shape of steel will be formed. The excess must be cut out or it will form a weak spot. Where there is an overlap this should be from 16 ins.—24 ins.

The concrete is delivered by a mobile rig in-cluding a large (and noisy) compressor, a mixer and a hose up to 200 ft. long with a nozzle where the dry gunite mix (1 : 4½) is combined with water and blown through the steel against the walls and floor of the excavation. (The largest size of aggregate used should be ⅜ in.)

The minimum standards of concrete thickness are 4½ ins. walls, 4 ins. floor and 7 ins. at corners or stress points. Because of irregularities in the excavation, the walls and floor are usually 6 ins. thick. The ring bondbeam all around the top edge of the pool is 14 ins. deep and 12 ins. wide and the back is tapered down to the 6 ins. walls. The beam is heavily reinforced with three or four bars of ⅝ in. deformed high-tensile steel. The mix blasts out of the nozzle at a speed of some 400 ft. per sec. and forms a very dense waterproof pool shell. However, the soundness of the shell depends upon the expertise of the nozzle operator. The shell must be of uniform thickness. All rebound (loose gunite mix that falls from the walls or nozzle) must be swept up as it forms weak pockets. (Rebound forms a very good base for paving and can be shovelled out into prepared areas.)

Slump occurs when the mix is too wet. Should

a section of wall collapse, the gunite must be cut away and the section built up with fresh layers. Voids could form a weak spot behind the steel bars if care is not taken to get the mix behind the bars. All inlets and pipes should have the ends covered so that they do not become filled with gunite.

In wet conditions the walls of the excavation should be lined with viscoene plastic sheeting to prevent hydraulic pressure pushing water through the gunite before it is set and carrying the cement away to leave a weak spot consisting of plain aggregate. If any such spots occur they should be plugged with a special quick-setting mix.

The shell is then finished with a waterproof render, an 8 ins. tile band under the coping, and then a $\frac{1}{4}$ in.—$\frac{5}{8}$ in. coat of Marbelite, or paint.

Concrete steps can be formed in the shallow end by the gunite crew, or later by finishers using blocks or hard bricks.

The advent of gunite and the dry pack method (described in paragraph 8) has made it feasible to produce pools of every imaginable shape.

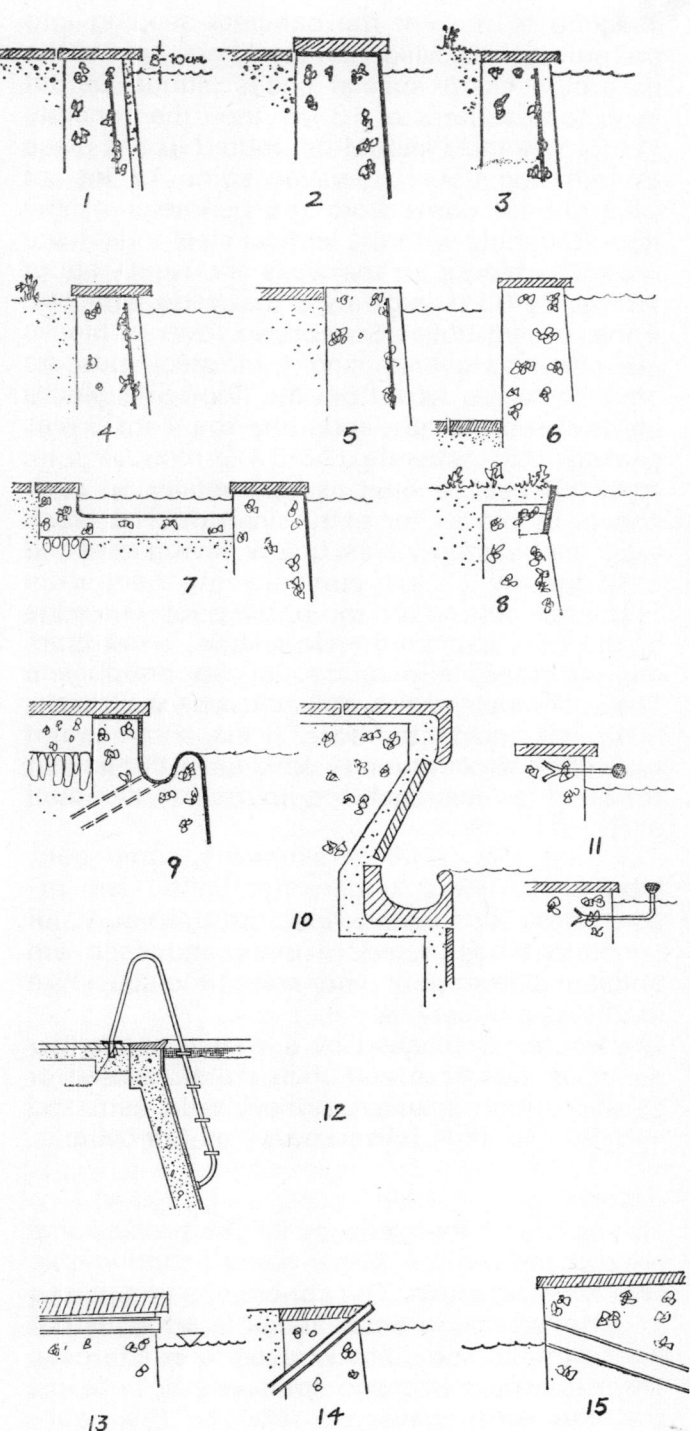

1. edging level with paved surround
2. edging one paving-stone higher
3. edging level with grass
4. edging one paving-stone higher than grass
5. pool without edging and level with paving
6. trough-type pool with high water level
7. foot-bath made watertight with elastic skin
8. edging with concreted-in vitreous tiles
9. overflow channel made watertight with elastic skin
10. ceramic overflow channel
11. hand rails as high as possible
12. removable stainless steel steps
13. inlet below the edging but above the highest water level
14. groups of inlets as a fountain
15. overflow pipe set into the wall

8. Dry pack (or hand-packed) concrete pools

A special patented concrete formula is used for these pools, the texture of which, being highly plastic, allows the shell to be formed without the use of shuttering. The plasticisers produce a considerable amount of heat permitting construction to continue under light frost conditions. For all practical purposes it is impervious to water and any weepholes should be plugged before the finishes are applied.

Excavation, preparation and steeling are essentially the same as for gunite. The aggregate is larger, giving a very strong concrete. It is prepared at the nearest concrete plant, under good conditions, to a specification which is electronically controlled. The concrete is then delivered to site by lorry in 5 or 6 yard loads, to be put into the pool. Here a team of six to eight men form the pool by tossing the concrete against the sides of the excavation, building up the walls and forming the ring bondbeam and floor. The minimum thicknesses are 8 ins. for the wall and 6 ins. for the floor, increased according to depth and ground conditions. The stiff mixture can be easily contoured and formed before it hardens.

Water

Swimming pool water should be kept clear and free from bacteria, animal or vegetable growth either by emptying, cleaning and refilling the pool, or by the use of chemicals.

Various forms of chlorine are used to sterilize and one should always ensure that the preparation used includes cyranuric acid, since the addition of this acid inhibits the destructive effect of sunlight on chlorine which will, therefore, last longer. Chlorine can be pumped automatically into the pool or added by hand, in liquid, powder or large tablet form. Algae, which are fast-growing spores, are countered by super-chlorination aided by an algicide. Iodine and bromine are also used for sterilizing but have never become popular owing to difficulty in control and handling.

Sterilization of water is now quite frequently done without chemicals, which have a smell and can affect the asthma-prone. Electrolysis is expensive to install but cheaper to run. Minute positively-charged ions of silver and copper are introduced into the water, which prevent the growth of bacteria and vegetable matter. The system is automatically controlled by a time-clock. (See illus. 88b.)

A test kit to show the P.H. (Potential Hydrogen Ions) condition and chlorine content of the water is an essential. Neutral water has a P.H. value of about 7·4. The water should be prevented from becoming too acid or alkaline since this can result in sore eyes, lips, etc., and can also impair the action of the chlorine. A variety of good chemicals in liquid or powder form is available and full instructions come with the preparations.

Other water problems such as hardness (which forms deposits on walls as in a kettle) or iron content (which forms brown stains) are best referred to a water board expert or to the pool builder.

Filtration
Dust and debris

This problem, caused by leaves, blossoms, atmospheric pollution, etc., can be put in three categories:

1. Fine debris in suspension in the water is extracted from the outlet by a filter with its power plant in the form of a pump (the sump is at the bottom and the skimmers at water level). Clean water is returned via the inlets. The inlets are set so as to drive the water in a circular motion, straight across or down the length of the pool to help the skimmer action.

2. Floating debris used to be cleared by constructing an overflow channel all around the pool which serves as a handrail at the same time. Expense can be saved by having the channel along one side of the pool only, preferably the side towards which insects, leaves, etc., will be driven by the prevailing wind.

Automatic skimmers are the efficient modern

method of clearing the water surface and avoid one of the disadvantages of overflows, namely the formation of algae in inaccessible channels. These skimmers consist of a 6 ins. opening in the wall of the pool under the edge of the paving. The water is drawn in by suction from the filter plant and the leaves are trapped in a basket. Floating weirs adjust to a variation in the water level of about 4 ins.

Overflows are necessary in ornamental pools but not in swimming pools where algae and other growths are unacceptable.

Removal of this surface debris is particularly important since the fine oily scum which forms on the top of the water cannot be reached by chlorine and, experts maintain, can be a source of infection.

3. Debris lying on the floor of the pool is collected by a water vacuum driven by the pump. It consists of a suction head on wheels which rolls along the bottom of the pool sucking up the heavy debris. This passes along a hose coupled to a point connected to the pump, where a strainer basket traps the larger pieces and the small particles are trapped in the filter.

An automatic robot (see illus. 88b) is now available which moves continually around the pool. A jet of water from the top sprays and cleans the walls above water level and the surface of the water, causing debris to sink. Two constantly moving hoses attached to the robot move about the pool: one cleans the bottom and directs larger pieces of debris to a removable basket, the other cleans the walls. All the fine debris is kept in suspension and can be removed by the filter.

Filters

A private swimming pool should have a turnover of ten hours or less. This means that the contents of the pool (10,000 or 20,000 gallons) should pass through the filter in that time. Semi-public pools usually have a turnover of six hours, public pools two to four hours.

The filter media most commonly used are sand and diatomaceous earth. Diatomaceous earth removes particles as small as two microns and has a polishing effect on the water, giving it a sparkle. The diatomaceous earth in the filter, however, has to be renewed regularly, sometimes even weekly, and the fabric septums on some filters have to be cleaned at intervals, with acid.

High-rate sand filtration takes slight preference since the sand does not need to be changed for years and the system lends itself to automatic backwashing, a method by which the debris collected in the filter is washed away to waste in a drain or soakaway.

When filtering, the water passes from the top of the tank down through the filter bed so that the debris is trapped and the cleaned water passed back to the pool. The filter can be cleaned (backwashed) by manipulating a single valve. The water then enters into the bottom of the tank and the dirt is flooded out of the filter bed to waste.

Much interesting work is being done with other filter media, particularly with permanent media where new substances, including plastics, are giving better results. Work is also being done on electrostatic filters though none has yet reached the production stage.

Heating

The addition of a heating system immediately makes a pool pleasanter and more serviceable.

The cost of the plant is usually slightly more than putting central heating in a house. The running cost is, however, less for the period from the beginning of May to the end of September, and even into November. Average temperatures are 22°C to 27°C. Heaters should be capable of raising the temperature by 2°C per hour.

The basic sources of heat are the sun, oil, town gas, electricity, butane gas, coal, or heat pumps.

Solar Heaters

These have a small pump which circulates the water through large heat exchangers, usually copper, under glass. In temperate climates an additional booster is necessary.

Oil Heating
This is usually done by pressure jet boilers. The wall flame type of boiler is not designed for the sustained demands made by a swimming pool. Oil is cheaper to run but can be noisy and may smell at times, also an oil tank is needed. The plant should be sited down-wind where possible.

Town Gas Heating
This method is quieter but more expensive to run than oil heating. A gas supply must be provided which could mean a new mains if the supply is not sufficient.

Electric Heating
This can be as much as double the price of town gas. However, it is very efficient since none of the heat is wasted; it is silent and the problems are few. It can prove economic for indoor pools where the building is already centrally heated.

Butane Gas Heating
Since tanks have replaced bottles as the means of storage, this form of heating is now comparable in price to heating by town gas. The newly developed boilers are becoming less costly than those for town gas or oil.

Coal and Solid Fuel Heating
This type of boiler cannot be turned on and off so is not suitable for use on a swimming pool unless also used on a house heating system. An indirect heat exchange system must be installed since no rust from the house pipes must enter the pool. To be effective it must run at 80°C.

Heat Pumps
Heat can be extracted from water or the air and passed to the pool, but the equipment now available is not capable of achieving high temperatures. (The most interesting example of this is the Festival Hall in London which extracts heat from the Thames.) The process is simply the reverse of that used in a refrigerator where heat is extracted.

Heat Retention Chemicals
Chemicals added every five to ten days which increase the surface tension of the water and form a very thin, invisible layer can reduce losses of heat radiation and evaporation: heated pools steam visibly on cool evenings. The cost would be ten to fifteen pence a week and would save one third, or more, of fuel costs.

All pool builders give special instructions for winter care of swimming pools. These vary with the construction and type of pipework used, and should be carefully followed to avoid damage by frost and ice.

Underwater Lights
Underwater lighting can create a particularly beautiful effect, illuminating from below the immediate area of the pool with a soft glow. It is also an important safety factor. Most underwater lights are low voltage (12 volts) and fitted into wall niches; they should be fitted and connected by an expert. The average 30 to 36 ft. pool would need a 12 volts 300 watt (6,000 lumens) safety light, calculated on $\frac{3}{4}$ watt per square foot of surface area.

Architects and Pool Consultants

Front cover pool W. Beresford Hales
Back cover pool R. H. S. Wisely

1 G. Lüttge, Hamburg
2 O. Valentien, Thumen
3 P. Darius, Stuttgart
4 O. Valentien, Thumen
6 Design: H. Steinbrenner
7 R. Weber, Düsseldorf
8 Design: Biedenkopf College
9 H. Birkigt, Düsseldorf
10 R. Weber, Düsseldorf
11 G. Lüttge, Hamburg
12 M. Gross, St Gallen
14 F. Vogel, Berne
15 R. Weber, Düsseldorf
17 F. Vogel, Berne
18 R. Willumeit, Darmstadt
19 H. Birkigt, Düsseldorf
20 H. Thiele, Unterwolkersdorf
22 O. Valentien, Thumen
23 V. Calles, Köln
25 R. Haag, Stuttgart
26 R. Willumeit, Darmstadt
27 V. Calles, Köln
28 H. Thiele, Unterwolkersdorf
30 G. Lüttge, Hamburg
31 G. Boye, Copenhagen
32 Carl-Axel Acking, Stockholm
33 H. Kindermann, Karlsruhe
34 W. Böninger and P. Diedermann, Munich
35 H. Kühn, Lübeck
36 H. Kühn, Lübeck
37 H. Kühn, Lübeck
39 H. Kühn, Lübeck
40 G. A. Jellicoe & Partners, London
42 Richard J. Neutra with B. Fischer, S. Koschin, J. Blanton, Los Angeles
44 Richard J. Neutra with B. Fischer, S. Koschin, J. Blanton, Los Angeles
45 H. Birkigt, Düsseldorf
48 A. Haag, Stuttgart
49 A. Seifert, Munich
50 G. Lüttge, Hamburg
51 E. Jörgensen, Copenhagen
52 W. Egli, Stäfa/Switzerland
55 Hans Kammerer and Walter Belz, Stuttgart
56 G. Lüttge, Hamburg
57 G. Lüttge, Hamburg
58 P. Schönholzer, Riehen/Basel
60 P. Schönholzer, Riehen/Basel
61 Richard J. Neutra with B. Fischer, S. Koschin, J. Blanton, Los Angeles
62 O. Valentien, Thumen
63 L. Roemer, Söcking
65 A. Bachmann & Söhne, Winterthur
66 W. Lurz, Stuttgart
67 P. Schönholzer, Riehen/Basel
68 G. Heydenreich, Hanover
69 Walter and Klaus Leder, Zurich
70 Richard J. Neutra with B. Fischer, S. Koschin, J. Blanton, Los Angeles
71 O. Schuberth, Weilheim
72 A. Bachmann & Söhne, Winterthur
73 R. Willumeit, Darmstadt
74 Richard J. Neutra with B. Fischer, S. Koschin, J. Blanton, Los Angeles
75 R. Homann, Bremen
76 F. Ruempler, Köln
77 O. Valentien, Thumen
78 G. Lüttge, Hamburg
79 W. Böninger and P. Biedermann, Munich
80 A. Haag, Stuttgart
81 A. Haag, Stuttgart
83 Walter and Klaus Leder, Zurich
84 V. Calles, Köln
85 H. Richard, Zurich
86 St Legge, U. Legge-Suwelack, Laumersdorf
87 C. F. Raue, Munich
88a F. C. Gold, London
88b E. Collett, Surrey
89 F. Gorian, Montevideo
90 St Legge, U. Legge-Suwelack, Laumersdorf
91 A. Haag, Stuttgart
92 K. Karnatz, Trier
94 P. Porcinai, Florence
95 Pierre Koenig, Los Angeles
96 H. Stoffer, Berne
98 K. Karnatz, Trier
99 L. Roemer, Söcking
100 E. Collett, Surrey and J. E. Grant-White, Brighton
101 Richard Neutra, Los Angeles
103 F. A. Breuhaus de Groot, Köln
104 Gilliam & Co. Ltd., London

105 K. Karnatz, Trier
106 H. Groethuysen, Munich
107 P. Porcinai, Florence
108 H. Thiele, Unterwolkersdorf
109 Richard J. Neutra with
B. Fischer, S. Koschin,
J. Blanton, Los Angeles
110 P. Neufert, Köln
111 J. Schweizer, Basel
112 Richard J. Neutra with
B. Fischer, S. Koschin,
J. Blanton, Los Angeles
113 K. Ackermann, Munich
114 K. Plomin, Hamburg
115 F. Ruempler, Köln
116 R. Weber, Düsseldorf
117 G. Lüttge, Hamburg
119 R. Willumeit, Darmstadt

List of Photographers

Th. Andresen, Copenhagen, 21, 46, 51, 64, 119
Archiv, 33, 35, 36, 37
A. Brugger, Stuttgart, 3, 25, 48, 80, 81, 91
Catling, Sevenoaks, Kent, 104
Ebert, Munich, 5
R. Eimke, Düsseldorf, 112
W. Ehmann, Köln, 76, 116
Engler, Winterthur, 72
Eternit AG, Niederurnen, 53
J. Geissler, Köln, 27, 84
G. Gereardi, Nuremberg, 13
J. E. Grant White, Brighton, back cover, 88a, 88b, 100
H. Hahn, Münchengladbach, 7, 10, 117
Handford Ltd., London, front cover
P. Hübotter, Hanover, 34
Jansen, Zurich, 69, 83
Kägi, Stäfa, 52
A. Löhndorf, Basel, 111
Niederhauser, Berne, 96
O. Rheinländer, Hamburg, 1, 30, 56, 57, 78, 118
L. Roemer, Söcking, 63, 99
Ch. Rohrback, Berlin, 102
I. v. d. Ropp, Köln, 23, 79
H. Schmölz, Köln, 16, 114
J. Shulman, Los Angeles, 42, 43, 44, 70, 74, 110, 113
A. Seifert, Munich, 49, 55
H. Tschirren, Berne, 14
O. Valentien, Thumen, 2, 4, 22, 62, 77
H. Wagner, Hanover, 68
R. Winkler, Munich-Stuttgart, 86
Wolgensinger, Zurich ,15

Picture section. Bird baths 34. Wells and water troughs 38. Fountains 42. Water gardens 51. Ornamental pools 52. Pools for water plants 56. Swimming pools 69. Natural ponds and streams 92.

Small bird baths at the edge of the lawn or the terrace, with low shrubbery. **1** and **2,** flat basins hewn out of stone with wide edges for the birds to perch. **3** A flat earthenware bowl on the paved surround of a small fountain. **4** A sunken brick-built bath with stones to provide shallower water.

3

4

5

Free forms are also possible provided the character of the stone employed is preserved. **5** A smoothly-hewn block of marble with a small fountain as water inlet. **6** A smoothly-formed basin of marble lying in the grass. **7** Glacier ice and weathering have sculptured this bizarre form. **8** A roughly-worked stone with sculptured decoration.

6

7

8

Watering tubs for the flower and vegetable garden have an advantage over the hose and garden spray in that they always provide temperate water. **9** A simple wooden tub, a halved barrel, sited where most often needed. It is filled with a hose and, to avoid mud, surrounded by dry paving. **10** A comparatively expensive container with a surrounding of Dutch bricks and a fixed inlet of bent water-pipe. The overflow is connected to the drainage system.

An old draw-well, **13,** and, **12,** a trough made out of a hollowed tree trunk retain their simplicity. A small water-trough made of concrete, **11,** faced with natural stone is suitable for public gardens. The base is indented and there is a coping of stone slabs. Drainage here is into a soakaway.

39

14

15

16

17

The shape and location of water troughs and drinking fountains are open to endless variations. In spite of the difference in type, the examples on these two pages are, above all, functional. The water-trough, **14,** receives reflected warmth from the wall. The surround is of stone. The trough in **17** is incorporated in a wall and the small drinking fountain, **15,** consists of a roughly-hewn stone which together with the surrounding rocks forms the boundary between lawn and play area. **16** An old stone water-trough surrounded by low shrubbery.

18

19

20

42

Five fountains with round basins but otherwise completely different. **18** A sunken basin framed by natural stone in a paved yard which is broken up by the use of low planting. A trough, **20,** reminiscent of the old fountains in city squares. **19** A deep basin of stone standing in the open and, **21,** a similar one constructed out of thick wooden planks. **22** A charming small basin with external water jets.

21

22

23 and **24** show a fountain with no noticeable surround. The edges of the sloping base stand just above the surrounding paving which is of the same type of stone, thus avoiding a dark expanse of water. **25** Some water plants will survive in the turbulent waters of a fountain but they should only be planted around the edge where they will not detract from the effect.

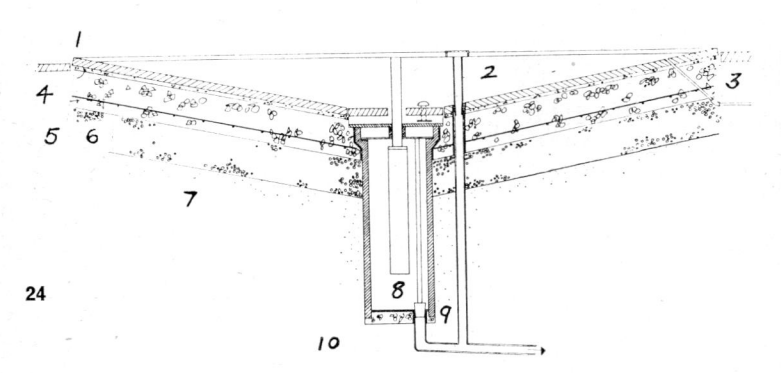

23

24

1. paving
2. pipe set on top of cone
3. reinforcement
4. concrete
5. concrete
6. cinders
7. earth
8. pipe fitted in concrete
9. bitumen waterproofing
10. outlet pipe 5 cm

(1cm = $\frac{3''}{8}$)

25

26 The water lies at the deepest part of the garden in the soft outlines of a semi-natural pond. The only division between the land and the water is a thin line of stones. This is an arrangement which is very simple but requires a feeling for shape and form to give the impression of a miniature landscape. **27** A fountain basin which resolves into a little stream running through the planting.

28

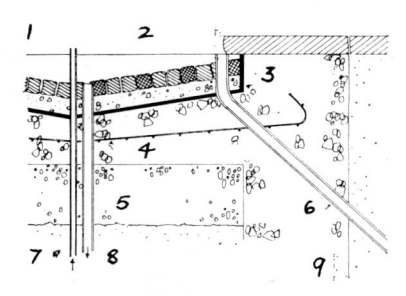

29
1. fountain
2. overflow with filter
3. double layer of bitumen waterproofing 1·5 cm.
4. reinforcing steel
5. gravel
6. overflow 38 mm
7. inlet 19 mm
8. outlet 38 mm
9. foundations on firm ground at least 80 cm.

(1cm = 3/8")

Two attractive possibilities for incorporating a fountain in a paved area. **28** and **29** This square shape set in a regularly paved area is laid with different coloured stones arranged in circles. The small sitting area, **30**, contains this eight-sided, slightly raised, fountain in one corner.

30

46

31

32

Fountains in groups. Round basins, **31,** on a large area of lawn and square basins, **32,** which, together with flower beds of the same size, are surrounded by paving.

Water as a lively element in the garden can, as in this example from Brussels, **33,** flow almost inaudibly over round pebbles and soak away into the gravel below. **34** The trickling sound of small fountains can also be an added attraction.

35

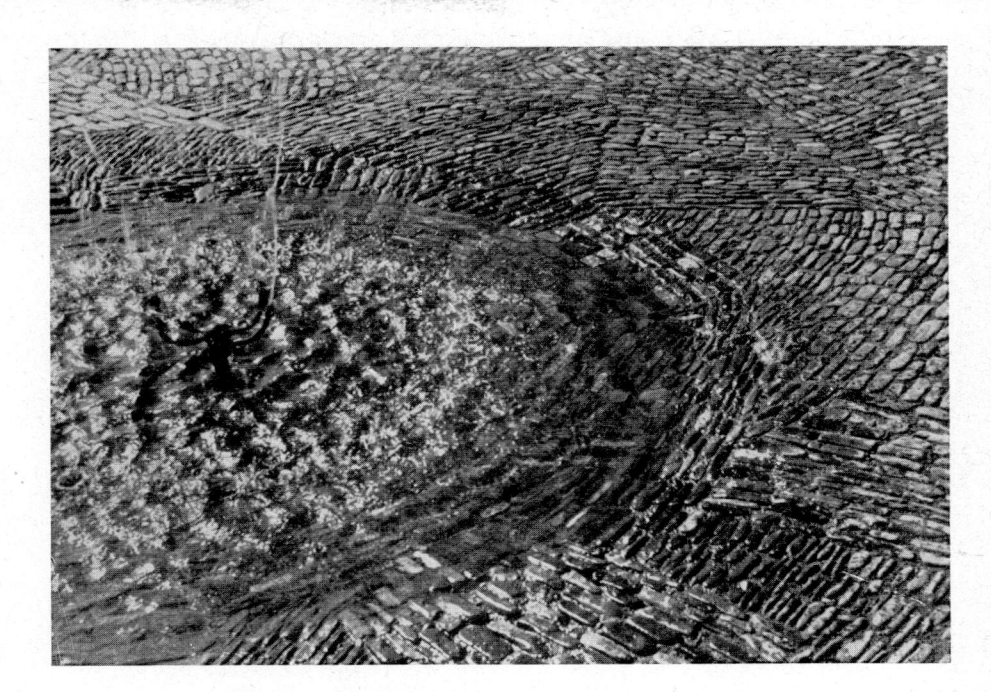

A rotating movement can also be soothing, as shown by these fountains at Lübeck. A shallow depression in the cobblestones, **35,** a pebbled hollow adjoining a pathway of crazy paving as in **37,** or the flat concrete basin painted with waterproof colours with a brick surround, **36,** are only a few of the types of suitable pools for rotating water jets.

36

37

Two other possibilities for fountains. **38** Old millstones set on top of one another in a shallow basin with rotating water jets add liveliness and beauty to the water garden. **39** A small fountain with fixed jets and curving water sprays is an attractive alternative. The structure of the basin is similar to that in picture **36**.

38

39

40

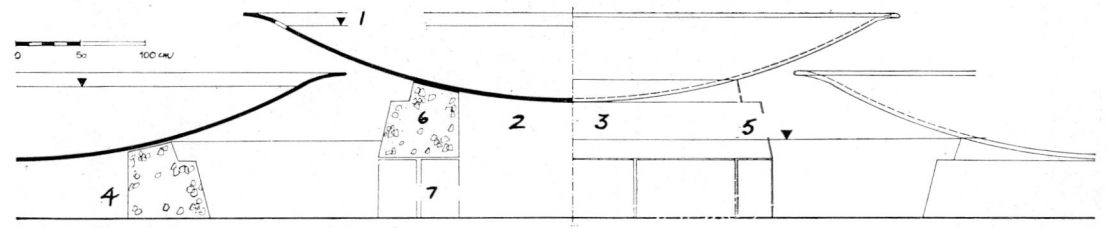

41
1. water level
2. cross section
3. side view
4. concrete
5. water level in the large pool
6. concrete
7. brick wall

A water garden with terraces on different levels, steps, bordering flower beds, stepping-stones and fountains. This is situated on the roof of a large department store, but could as easily be incorporated into a quiet corner of a large garden.

51

42 America has re-discovered reflecting pools: large, flat water surfaces which mirror the house or the landscape. To derive their full effect, reflecting pools should be constructed in the grand manner. In hot climates, the shallow pool by the house is particularly welcome for cooling the hot air. **43** Pools in which plants and fishes provide a biological equilibrium are easier to keep clean. The round stepping stones and the large piece of rock in its surround make a distinct and pleasing contrast to the straight sides of the pool. **44** The view of the pool from the house is too often neglected but should be an important factor.

42

43

44

45

46

47

Water can be confined in many ways as a decorative and constructive element in the garden. The small dark pool in which the grasses and shrubs are reflected, **45,** or those decorated with figurative designs, **47,** are very suitable for small layouts and are not expensive. The artificial water-course, **48,** emphasized as such by its shape and concreted channel, has the effect of an elegant arabesque on this smooth slope. Only an expert, however, can ensure that the freedom of material and form are not abused.

48

49

50

51

Lily-ponds in severe rectangular form, surrounded by natural stone with normal **(49, 51)** or low-lying **(50)** water levels, are in keeping with architectural surroundings. They can be framed partly by high-growing shrubs and in fact the bigger they are the bolder their surroundings must be in relation to the house or the garden.

52

53

Both these small pools are prefabricated 'Eternit' baths which are manufactured in different sizes and can also be used as paddling pools. No waterproofing is necessary and only a covering for the outer rim need be provided if this latter is firmly built. The outlet pipe can be connected directly to a soakaway or the drainage system although this may not always be necessary.

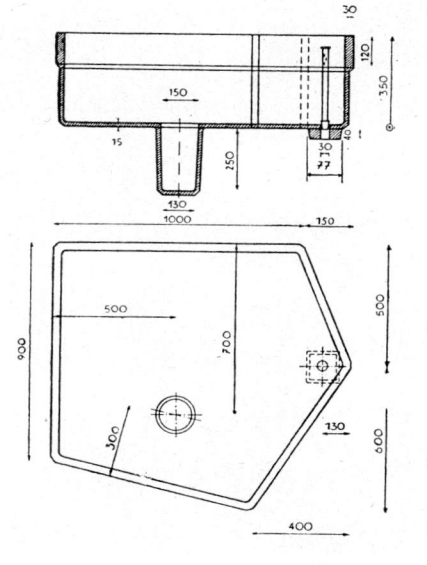

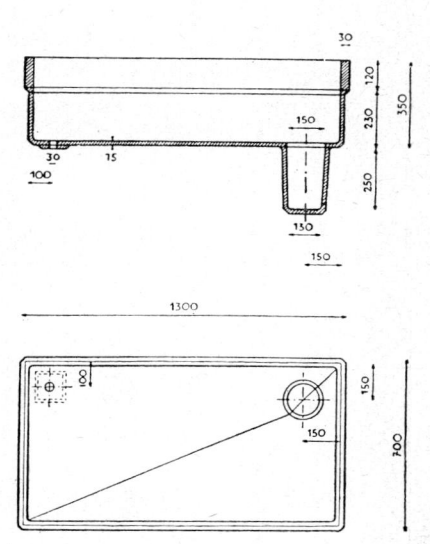

(1cm = ⅜")

54

55 The pool in this patio is lined with the same stones as the surrounding paving and the accent is on the more classical form with the use of sculpture, pebbles and various plants. **56** This pool borders on the lawn, a terrace paved with cobbles and a small slope from which it is divided by a low wall. **57** This pool and the two previous examples show the tremendous range possible in the relationship between pool and environment.

57

58

59

60

The final effect of a pool also depends on how it is planted. Whether the plants are to grow freely, which makes the water surface appear smaller, or whether they are to be concentrated at one particular point, must be taken into consideration in the planning.

The contrast between a sharply defined, almost crystalline structure of a house and a freer, more artistic pool form, can be very effective. The water surface itself is free of plants but they flourish beautifully behind the edging of stones. This unusual conception of keeping the water, plants and buildings separate is satisfactory only when there is plenty of space and an abundance of plants available.

61

62

63

62, 63 and **64** show how pools can be incorporated with the surrounding structures. Pergola, house, garden, hedge or wall are all means of creating an effect in which the pool is a necessary, even dominant, part. Even in the open, **65,** an orderliness must be maintained if one part of the layout is not to detract from another.

64

65

66

These three small pools show further variations on this theme. **66** The pool is set in the paving near the door, with a surround of removable wooden plants. **67** In these two pools the water flows in a thin stream into the larger one. **68** A small pool in the lawn with a narrow edging of stone.

67

68

69 Gardens which border on a lake or within sight of one should always have pools which are obviously 'built', so that they do not look like a miniature lake themselves. The ground-plan can vary according to circumstances but the pool should be outlined with stones or plants in such a way that it remains a real part of the garden.

1. Japanese fan-maple
2. bog plants
3. walnut
4. drainage

69

70

The effect of water, house and plants either complementing one another or forming a contrast can be realised on a large or more intimate scale. A large layout should not be spoilt by fussy details but viewed as a whole, whereas a smaller layout will obtain its effect mainly from good detail. In the latter case, careful use of resources and choice of plants are particularly important.

71

72

Two swimming pools in conjunction with buildings. **73** A covered-in area for deck-chairs which provides privacy and shelter from the wind. **74** The swimming pool immediately adjoining the house. Whereas in the first case the pool can be located anywhere in the garden, in the lower picture it is the focal point of the living area.

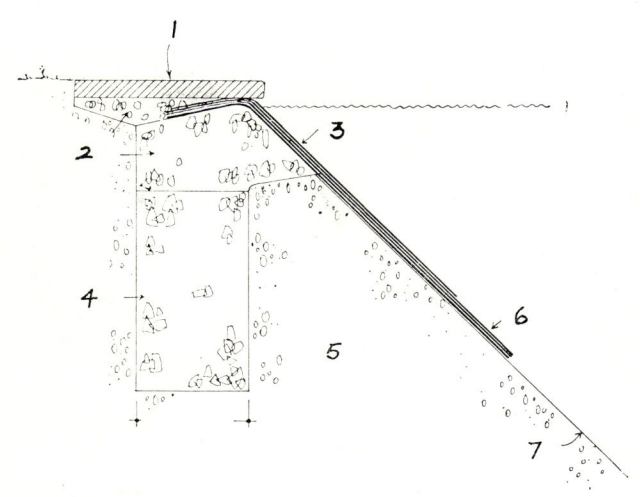

1. coping
2. concrete
3. single layer of roofing felt as lining
4. concrete
5. solid earth
6. 3 layers of roofing felt
7. soil surface cleanly smoothed off

75 **76**

75 In contrast, a very simple swimming pool, the water surface of which is an integral part of a strictly systematically arranged garden. Such a reasonably-priced structure will last for years, with proper care. The reinforced concrete pool, **76,** lies to one end of the house and is therefore out of the normal field of view, although still connected to the house by the covered terrace. In such cases, the terrace should not be the only means of access to the garden.

77

78

A plateau on a hillside makes a good situation for this swimming pool, **77,** which is protected from the wind and also benefits from the view. The pool is placed right up against the wall and is joined to the house by paving and steps. **78** A completely different setting, the corner of a walled garden. **79** A swimming pool in an enclosure, thoughtfully arranged with wooden duck-boards, areas of paving and patches of pebbles with a few plants. Awnings can be stretched between the beams.

79

The circular swimming pool lies at the edge of a park-like garden. Its form is further emphasized by the path leading round it, the low wall and the semi-circular bank behind it. Round pools of this size are also suitable for swimming. The similarity between the topographical situation and the shape of the pool create a particularly harmonious effect.

The L-shape of this pool has been designed with the shape of the ground and the position of the house in mind. Against the background of trees on the boundary of the garden, areas of planting have been laid out with benches for sitting. The wider part of the pool is level with the middle terrace so as not to detract from the effect of a large lawn. A less formal outline can be as effective, provided the components of the garden are arranged to fit in with each other.

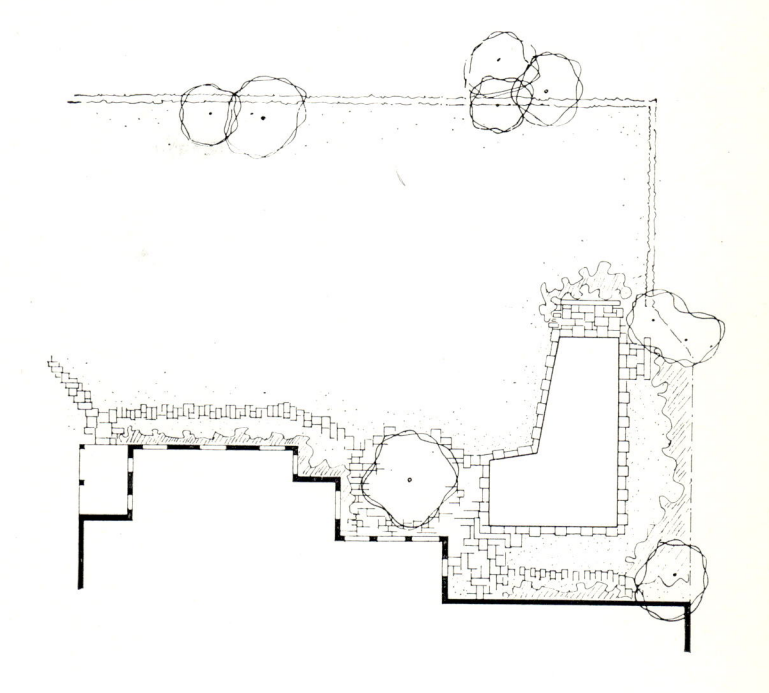

84

85

These two pictures show different ways in which steps can be arranged with pools, without having to lead directly to them. **86** The problem of a link between the swimming pool and living accommodation on a higher level is solved quite differently. The open stairway is accompanied by a shallow pool and leads to a paved terrace at the side of the swimming pool. **87** A strictly geometrical relationship between house and pool which are connected by a raised terrace.

86

87

88a

88b

89

90

91

Two English pools. **88a** From Mickleham, Surrey, this is a monolithic construction made from plasticized concrete, steel reinforced, with high-rate sand filtration, oil heating and sterilization by chlorine. The design won the American Swimming Pool Age award; the york-stone walling with planting cavities is particularly suitable for a pool where one end is out of ground. **88b** From Cobham, Surrey, house, garden, pool and raised circular flower bed integrate well. The wall on the left screens changing rooms and forms a windbreak. This pool has high-rate sand filtration, town gas heating, electrolytic sterilization, and a Robot pool cleaner which can be seen in the water. **89** In South America, this pool has a free form but is given shape by the use of long-established trees and groups of planting. **90** The pool runs partly underneath the house, the projecting part being divided off with stepping stones. There is an approach to the upper storey by means of the outside steps. **91** A round pool closely bordered by plants.

92

93

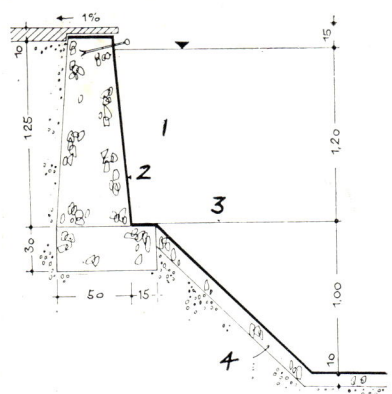

(1cm = $\frac{3}{8}$″)

1. 10° batter
2. plastic lining
3. ledge
4. 10 cm thick sloping bottom

These pools also have an ungeometrical ground form. They are not cramped or stylised because of their size and position. **93** The gradual slope below the ledge reduces costs without interfering with the swimming. A steep drop is constructed immediately below the diving-board, only.

94

79

95

96

1. inlet
2. overflow
3. outlet
4. to drainage
5. bed of stones

97

80

98

Paths, walls, covered terraces and steps can all be effective in incorporating the pool into the garden. In **95** and **96,** tiered terraces and dwarf walls are used to bring together the technical and functional parts of the pool so that the greater part of it can be joined to the garden by means of planting, or areas of lawn. Open summer-houses, **97,** should be as far from the house as possible, especially in bigger gardens, to create a second point of interest. **98** The pool is set in an angle in the house and becomes the focal point of outdoor living. Open and covered terraces provide sheltered places in all weathers.

99

100

99 A narrow piece of ground of modest dimensions appears larger than it is because of its spacious arrangement, contrasting with the close proximity of house and pool. 100 Swimming pool in a London garden at Holland Park. Both the alcove of the fountain and the interior of the swimming pool are finished in various tones of blue Italian glass mosaics. 101 A very attractive layout but only practical where the pool can be used for most months of the year. 102 A small detail: cylinders of cement filled with concrete and used as stepping stones. These would also be suitable for marking the boundaries between different depths.

101

102

83

103

The more a garden is open to the surrounding landscape, the less important the pool becomes as the centre of attention or the main motif in the garden; it becomes part of the scenery and should blend in as such. **103** In an enclosed garden the simple trapezoid is even more effective because of its correspondence in shape with the total area. **104** Outdoor pool in Farnham, Surrey. Shrubs have been planted to act as a decorative windbreak. **105** This is another example of plastic liner being used on the walls and base of a pool constructed from simple compressed concrete.

The two lower pictures on these pages show similar layouts achieved quite differently. **106** The clear-cut concrete outlines of the house with its well-defined divisions are reflected in the rectangular shape of the pool. Together they form a whole which projects into the surrounding parkland. **107** and **108** illustrate how swimming pools can be made to fit the garden space. In the upper picture, the side of the pool towards the house is straight while the other side follows the outlines of the rocks. **108** A very formal layout, an orderly relationship between house, steps, wall with pergola and the small dry wall which is timeless.

106

107

108

109 Such a view of the garden, pool and landscape beyond is possible only in a few countries but this example again demonstrates the importance of the view from the house.

109

110 A small swimming-pool connected to the house by means of terraces at different levels, bordering onto lawn and house areas. **111** The swimming pool continues inside the house as a shallow ornamental pool, under the roof. The inner and outer pools are separated by a thick pane of glass.

The pictures on these pages show how house and garden can be linked together. The swimming pool under the roof in **112** creates a formal, very intimate but spacious relationship between living and bathing, the garden and plants also giving the effect of being drawn into the house. The opposite case is the house which is dissociated from the existing pond, whose banks have been carefully planted but strengthened only on one side, **113**.

112

113

114

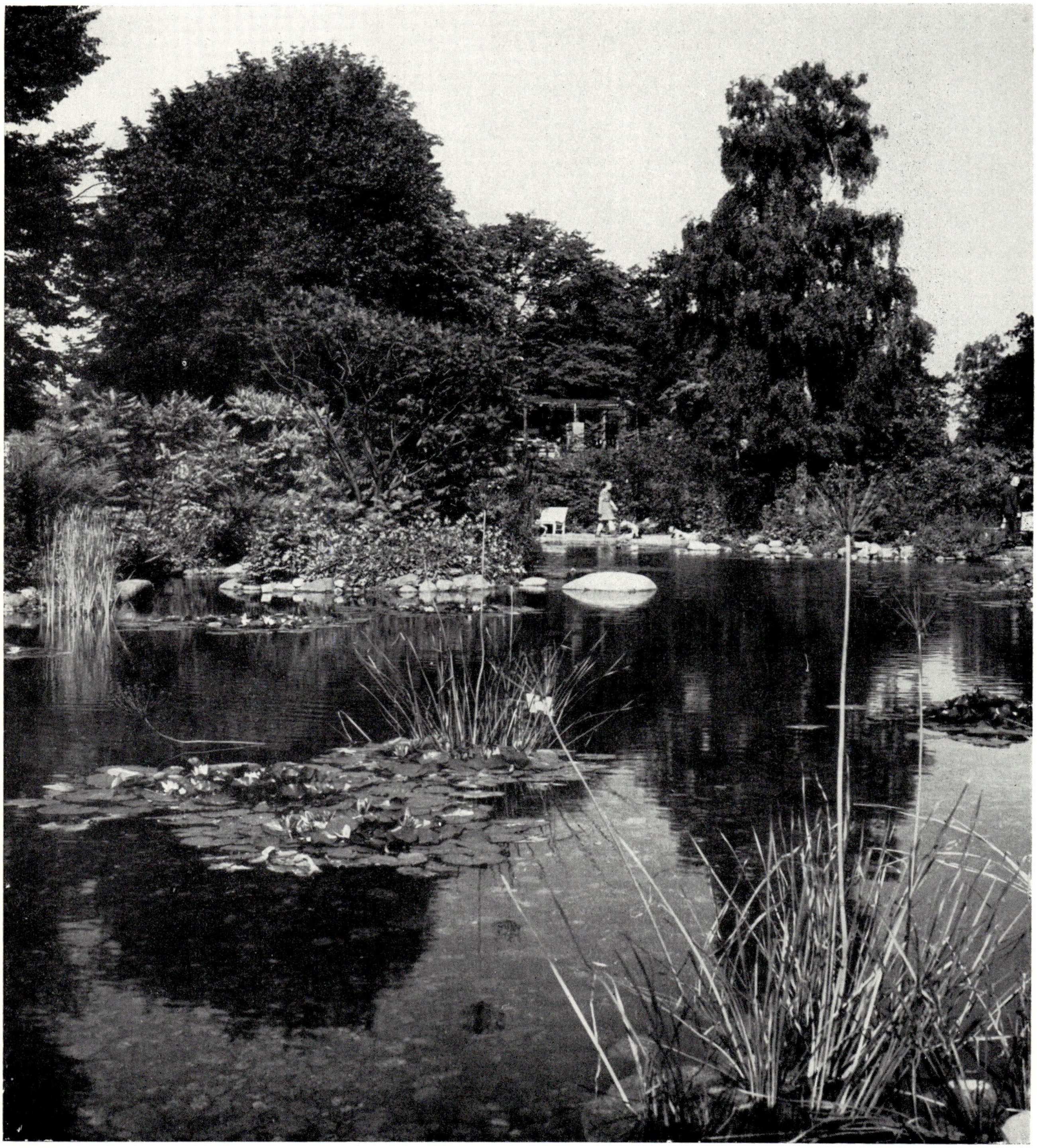

Even though natural ponds are a rarity in the garden, these pictures will provide some suggestions on how a large, continuous expanse of water can be adapted, how the banks can be planted and improved in an apparently natural way.

115

116

117

118

117 A small pond which was formerly just a water-hole but has been turned into an attractive and secluded spot through correctly chosen and placed planting. **118** A wide expanse of water forming part of a park in Denmark. It requires no details, apart from small alterations to the existing vegetation, to increase its effectiveness.

These are examples of small streams which have been confined and fitted into the garden scheme. **119** A natural spring which has been led underground and through a dry wall to form a small waterfall. **120** A brook which has been dammed up by a wall made of flat sandstone blocks, the top layer of which are laid at intervals so as to form a row of small waterfalls.